7 THINGS
YOU MUST KNOW
TO AVOID
FORECLOSURE
AND KEEP THE BANK
FROM TAKING
YOUR HOME

BARBARA ANN
SCHLINKER

FOREWORD

I want to tell you how great an advocate Barb is. I was pleased to hear that I could tell others facing the same problem just how life changing my help from Barb was. Barb's expertise in dealing with the bank and help with people struggling with their mortgage is unmatched! I was at the brink of a foreclosure. I had applied for a loan modification. The very same day my loan modification was approved, I received another lender from the same bank telling me my loan modification was denied. I owed much more on the home than it was worth. I did not have any money to pay the difference or pay an agent to sell my home. I had a mountain of debt, and did not know a way out of it. I found Barb at Parker St. Claire Realty online and was so glad I did. In just a few months, she was able to help me sell my home at no cost to me. Best of all, I will never have to pay back any unpaid debt. Her in-depth knowledge of how to deal with the bank, how to sell my home for free, and how to get out of all that debt has meant I can start over...even as a retired person! I continue to work toward rebuilding my credit so I can buy another home in a few short years. I am so pleased to write this foreword so you now can benefit from her expertise.

Mary F. Monument, Colorado

PREFACE

Seven years ago, I met with the first borrower who needed my help to sell his home and be relieved of his mortgage debt. His hardship was extraordinary. He had a gambling problem and had been released out of the military for his behavior. To make matters worse, he was discharged from the military on an "other than honorable" circumstance. After that, it was very difficult for him to find employment. Without income, there was no way he could obtain a loan modification or any repayment plan. He owed more on his home than it was worth and could not sell his home for enough to pay off the loan and the fees. Most buyers who viewed his home did not like that he had painted all of the beautiful clear-stained oak in the home flat black (which would scratch and chip off if you touched it). At the time, the real estate market was not that bad. However, he had borrowed more money than his home was currently worth, and he had no way to pay any of the closing costs or selling expenses such as commission. His lenders were very skilled at trying to get the buyer to pay more for the home, trying to get money from the agents, and trying to get the borrower to pay for debt he had no way of repaying. I learned so much on that transaction, and in the end, this young man was able to walk away from a mountain of debt and rebuild his life.

National statistics prove that most agents fail at helping people avoid foreclosure. Most real estate agents dislike helping borrowers in trouble because it is extra work above the normal real estate duties. Further, the approval process takes longer than a regular sale. Many real estate agents do not want to take their buyers to a short sale (which usually represents some of the best deals on the market) because they do not want to wait months and are concerned banks will ultimately not approve the buyer's offer. Many of short sale requests fail because the listing real estate agents do not learn how to price homes correctly or how to negotiate with the banks.

Never would I have imagined in my real estate career that I would specialize in helping borrowers settle unpaid debt. However, with the current state of market affairs, over five million borrowers more than thirty days delinquent on their loans nationwide, I find myself doing just that—debt settlement—and I am proud to help borrowers out of tough, heartbreaking situations. I know that, in the short-term, it is challenging for those clients. However, in just a few short years, those same people who had to sell their home to avoid foreclosure can buy a home again at a lower price and with a lower interest rate.

After I helped my first homeowner who could no longer afford his home, I discovered I really needed more skills to help my clients. Well, my wish came true. At a conference put on by one of the top real estate trainers in the country, I met some nice young men who shared with me how to get all of my *short sales* (when a property is sold for less than is owed and the bank agrees to a discounted payoff) approved. They told me about Mr. Lee Honish, a former IndyMac senior loss mitigator who used to be the "tough guy" making collection calls to borrowers in default. As you may know, Indy Mac was taken over by the FDIC. As a result, thankfully for all of us, Mr. Honish then began a business training agents and advocates on how to successfully negotiate short sales with the banks and protect the borrowers from debt collection tactics that scare them into giving more than they should. Since that time, all of my short sales have been approved in record time, all of my borrowers have received approval letters that hold them unaccountable for paying back any unpaid debt, and those clients have had no out-of-pocket costs for my services. Best of all, I've even had some borrowers *get paid* $20,000 to sell their home on a short sale after missing payments for years. It is so nice to hear from my clients that they are surprised their short sales went so fast and easy. Without Mr. Honish's training and expertise, my success in helping people in trouble with their mortgage would not be as good. He is one of the people who inspired me to write this book. My hope and goal is that this information is helpful to those who need it.

Dedication

This book is dedicated to my late father, Armand J. Parker, who was a mentor, leader, and source of great inspiration throughout my life, and also initiated and built my real estate career. His strength and integrity, as well as his kind, loving support, are the reasons I am privileged to have the skills and desire to help people with their real estate solutions.

ACKNOWLEDGMENTS

This book was written as a result of many people and clients I have helped and learned from over the years. I would like to thank them all and make a special note of appreciation for:

1) Mr. Lee Honish – My Certified Default Advocate creator and coach. An unbelievably smart and creative entrepreneur who improves the lives of everyone he touches.

2) Mr. Steve Guzman – A San Diego–based colleague who gives away his success secrets and offers help to those who ask. His humor and business savvy that he willingly shares has helped hundreds of Certified Default Advocates all over the country. To put it in a "Steve-ism," he is "all about the mission and not the commission."

3) Ms. Diana Ortiz – A great friend and master event coordinator who has shared her excellent expertise in negotiating short sales, resulting in more of my clients avoiding foreclosure.

4) Mrs. Janie Howard – My colleague and a real estate superstar who has taught me how to help people and accomplish goals with kindness, grace, and superb customer service.

5) Mr. Mark Schlinker – My best friend, husband, and business partner who stands by me. He is the best editor, thanks to his lovely mom, Mrs. Nona Schlinker, a teacher and beautiful lady. And most of all, I appreciate Mark's special abilities to find humor in any situation and articulate what is really important and put it into perspective.

6) Mr. Max Schlinker – My kind and considerate son and fine young man—the reason I am here.

TABLE OF CONTENTS

CHAPTER 1

HOMEOWNERS HAVE MORE OPTIONS THAN THEY THINK

As a Certified Default Advocate who helps people facing fore-closure, I know it is one the most stressful things a home-owner can experience. It breaks my heart to read, according to DS News, a foreclosure agency called YouWalkAway.com conducted a survey of its clients to find that a staggering 78 percent of owners were walking away from their primary residences—and letting the bank foreclose on them. My goal with this book is to provide a better way for the future of those owners who, at times through no fault of their own, find them-selves facing a mountain of debt against their home they cannot repay. Homeowners in trouble who need help most often call their bank *first*—giving them private financial information that can be used against them by the bank that services their mortgage. The bank is just a debt collector whose client is not the homeowner with the loan but the investor who put up the money for their loan. Having walked in the shoes of a home-owner facing foreclosure, I know what it feels like to have the banks calling constantly, to be offered unworkable solutions such as "pay all the back payments now or nothing at all" (as banks often demand), and to be told foreclosure is just around the corner. In 2007 our financial world began to unravel. My husband and I had purchased 4 rental homes. We had assumed the market values would continue to increase and someday those homes would be paid off with the rental income coming in. All of the homes were fully rented and financed with about 90% of their value. I remember asking the lenders if we really qualified for those mortgages. They would say, sure and encourage us not to worry, "the market values will go up and we would just refinance before the current mortgage rate adjusted". After owning most of them for 2-3 years, our adjustable rate mortgages suddenly ballooned up (to nearly double what it previously was) and we found ourselves having to pay over $8000 per month *more* than we were receiving in rental income. It did not take very long before we started to miss payments and to make matters worse, the market values were declining below what we owed on those homes. We took action to sell all of those homes on a short sale. At the time, the banks seemed more motivated to foreclose than to approve a short sale. (Things have changed since then). The approvals for the short sales at the time took well over 6 months and we typically had to find new buyers when the ones who were waiting out the approval process - got tired of waiting. We sold 2 of the homes on short sales. One of the banks that approved a short sale reported the sale as a foreclosure on our credit report. On the 3rd home, the bank decided they would make more money if it foreclosed because of mortgage insurance – yet the home later sold for less than the offer of the short sale. Then on the 4th house we could not get the second mortgage holder to accept a payoff for less half of what was owed (they wanted $40,000). So the 4th home foreclosed. Now the second mortgage holder sends letters every year with a revised new balance that grows exponentially from the original balance. We can only hope for the 6 year period to expire (which gives lenders the right to sue us for unpaid debt – called deficiency judgment). This is true in Colorado and every state has different laws about whether lenders can sue for unpaid mortgage debt. Throughout the process, the banks would constantly call us, call our family members, break in and re-key the vacant homes to "protect the asset" and put us through continued humiliation both on the phone and in writing. Having had those personal experiences I made it my mission to help as many borrowers as I could to avoid foreclosure. Having a foreclosure has many negative tax and credit disadvantages. There are so many other options that allow home owners facing foreclosure a more dignified and less costly way to prevent the financial challenges of a foreclosure and start on the path back to financial health much sooner than just letting the bank control the homeowner's financial destiny. Homeowners facing foreclosure have more options and more control over the situation than they may think.

Borrowers facing a foreclosure are hit with so many foreign terms that seeking help can be very confusing and scary. I've structured this book so that homeowners in trouble can be armed with the right answers and know their options to make the best decisions for their family. The first step is to understand what all the terms mean.

A) WHAT IS A FORECLOSURE?

It is a right of the bank, your debt collector(s), to take the collateral—the house—when the mortgage debt (a mortgage loan) is unpaid. It is similar to an auto repossession when an auto loan is not paid. However, a foreclosure often takes longer. Most states have different procedures for repossessing a home in a foreclosure. In the state of Colorado, the state where my business is based, most foreclosures are conducted by the county public trustee, who is given the authority, directed by the banks, to foreclose (take back ownership of the home) after approximately 120 days of providing the homeowner and borrower notice of the foreclosure. This notice is called a Notice of Election and Demand.

How Soon Can the Bank Foreclose?

Knowing your state's foreclosure timeline is essential. Most borrowers have no idea how long they can be in their property after mortgage payments are missed.

Some think they must move shortly after the first missed payment, while others think it's much longer. The truth is it is depends on what state you are located in since foreclosure law varies state by state. You must first know whether your state is judicial or non-judicial.

Colorado lenders have the option of either process, judicial or non-judicial, depending on what is in your mortgage document. The reason has to do with whether or not a "power of sale" exists in the mortgage. The power of sale means the mortgage document recorded against the home has written authorization to give the lender the power to foreclosure through their representative, typically called the "trustee." What is unique about Colorado is the governor appoints a "public trustee" to carry out the foreclosure sale in each county. If there is no power of sale, they must use the judicial (court) process. In most cases, though, the non-judicial process through a public trustee sale is used.

In Colorado, it takes approximately 120 days to foreclose on a borrower after the Notice of Default (NOD) is served for residential homes. A Notice of Default (which comes from the county public trustee) typically will be issued as soon as three months after missing the first payment, though it could be as long as a year plus. Banks do have the option to extend the date of the foreclosure, and they often will if it is appropriately requested. That is one of the reasons you need an excellent agent and advocate, should you choose to do a short sale—to prevent the foreclosure sale from happening.

> *Case Study 1: The Loan Modification Hoodwink*
> *One of my Colorado clients was being told every week that his loan modification was "in-process," awaiting approval. Over that same period, their lender had filed for foreclosure. The foreclosure sale date had already been extended four months during this process. Finally, only thirty-six hours before the scheduled foreclosure sale, the lender told this borrower that his loan modification had been denied for over two months, that his home was going to foreclose the next day, and there was nothing he could do. That is when he called me for help. I was able to get in contact with the right people at the bank to extend the foreclosure sale date. I quickly got a buyer for his home, and in just six weeks, that short sale closed. This borrower received a letter fully releasing him from his mortgage debt and he is on the path to rebuilding his credit.*

It is important to understand what NOD (Notice of Default) means. A Notice of Default is the official notice that foreclosure has been filed, foreclosure is being pursued by the bank, and the clock is ticking. You should be notified if an NOD has been filed because you will receive a document in the mail, in person, or through a posting on the property's door from the county public trustee's office. You can also expect to get a variety of legal documents from your bank, which may look very threatening.

In some states, the foreclosure process may be as quick as a couple months. It is extremely important your Certified Default Advocate truly understands your state's time-line since that is really the timeline you are up against. Depending on your situation, you will now know how fast or slow you need to move to choose the right foreclosure alternative before the foreclosure sale date.

Can the Foreclosure Sale Date Be Delayed?

Yes, in some cases, the banks will extend the foreclosure sale date. However, the banks do not have to. Borrowers facing foreclosure should seek help from a Certified Default Advocate to help with extending the foreclosure sale.

What Happens If My House Is Foreclosed?

Public trustee sales (foreclosure sales) occur, in Colorado, on one day of the week at a specific time at the public trustee's office. Many real estate investors attend these sales to purchase an option to obtain the title to the fore-closed homes. However, most of those homes are not purchased at the sale and automatically become "bank owned" homes if no one bids on them. At that point, the former owner no longer owns the home.

Case Study 2: The Heartbreak of Losing the Family Home

As a Certified Default Advocate and real estate broker, I also list and sell homes that are already foreclosed. Recently, I met a nice lady who has six children and requested to come back to her home, after the locks had been changed, to get some of her things. The bank thought the former owners had moved because most items were gone and the utilities were turned off. The bank had to gain access, change the locks, and get the heat started to protect the property from freeze damage. I could sense her sadness from the moment we met. I let her in the home to get her things. As she began to tell me her story, we both shared tears when she expressed her humiliation of having lost the home to foreclosure. She told me it was her family home they'd bought brand-new and had remodeled and improved over the years. She had been forced to foreclose by the court ordering her former husband to stop paying the mortgage, and she could not afford the payments on her own.

What was ten times worse was the story she shared with me that happened before the foreclosure. This former owner had hired a "real estate broker" to sell the home. That broker failed to tell her about two offers that were enough to pay off her mortgage, give her money, and prevent the foreclosure. That real estate broker just told the buyer's agent that their offers were too low and did not present the offers to her seller. Not only is failure to present all offers a license law violation in any state, but it caused this nice lady the harm of having an unnecessary fore-closure on her credit report. This is a worst-case scenario of someone hiring a real estate "professional" who led that family right to foreclosure. This true story is an excellent example of why homeowners in trouble must seek out the services of a Certified Default Advocate, who can help with foreclosure prevention.

What are the Consequences of Letting My Home Foreclose?

- Potential loss of job
- Potential credit collection on the unpaid debt
- Potential tax liability on the unpaid debt
- Having to report a foreclosure on every credit and job application going forward, and/or
- Having to wait as long as seven years to buy your next home

Will Someone Kick Me Out of My Home for Missing Payments?

The short answer is no. Many folks have this fear. There are many choices and, usually, plenty of time. Although

I have heard of unsavory characters and banks telling homeowners in trouble that they had to get out as soon as the first few payments are missed, that is not only cruel, but it is false. The bank has to complete the foreclosure sale, and then they usually give the foreclosed-on borrower time to move and/or start the eviction process, which takes at least one month. I have seen it take as long as a year after foreclosure for the former owner to leave. However, the typical time from foreclosure to eviction is about ninety days. Most often, the banks will offer move-out money to people who have foreclosed and are still in the home called "cash-for-keys" to leave the home clean and undamaged with no personal property or trash left behind.

B) WHAT IS A DEFAULT?

This means the borrower has not paid the mortgage loan as agreed upon. If a mortgage payment is not paid within thirty days after it is due, the borrower is in default.

C) WHAT IS FORBEARANCE?

Forbearance is an option a borrower in default can request to make up missed payments. This option is typically offered by banks if the borrower has missed fewer than four payments. The bank will take the number of missed payments, divide it by a time period—usually six months—and allow the defaulted borrower to catch up the missed payments over time.

What Is a Lien?

A lien is a loan or debt leveraged against an asset, such as a house. Liens are typically recorded by the county as a debt leveraged on a home. Nearly all mortgage loans are liens placed on homes as debt against the home. When the home is sold, the lien must be paid off or settled so the next buyer can purchase the home.

The Different Types of Liens

When facing foreclosure or a short sale, it is so important to distinguish the different types of liens on your property. There is a lot of miscommunication and bad advice out there on this subject. It is *essential* that your Certified Default Advocate is knowledgeable on how to negotiate the settlement of liens on the sale of the home. Getting good advice about this subject may make the difference between walking away with no financial liabilities and having thousands of dollars of debt to repay after the home is sold.

First Mortgage Lien: This is the primary mortgage, or senior lien, on the property. As long as this lien is being "shorted," the bank who holds this first position lien will have more approval authority in terms of how much is paid out in total closing costs, including commission, taxes, title/attorney fees, buyer's requested loan closing costs, and how much will be allowed to pay the second mortgage, or junior lien, holders. Banks who hold first liens most likely issue the seller a 1099-C (cancellation of debt) as the bank's recourse for waiving unpaid debt. The issuance of a 1099-C is the bank's way of writing off the unpaid debt. The first lien position, or senior lien holder, is typically the foreclosing lien. This is also normally the larger dollar amount. The banks have a choice to issue a 1099-C (cancellation of debt) or to issue their settlement letter without waiving "deficiency" (meaning the debt could be collected in the future). The banks cannot do both. However, if the borrower hires an untrained real estate agent who does not know how to negotiate with the banks to ensure the borrower will not be held accountable to pay back the unpaid debt, it opens the door for the bank to do both—write off the debt *and* sell it to collectors. That is why it is so important to hire a Certified Default Advocate to handle a short sale.

Second Mortgage Lien: True second mortgages were commonly used during the previous boom years as a creative financing tool to allow buyers to avoid paying private mortgage insurance (PMI)—insurance for the banks to protect their investment from foreclosure loss. Creative financing and the use of first and second mortgages were highly prevalent during the early 2000s, when market values were climbing, and lending guidelines were very unrestrictive. Formerly, we would see more of these second mortgages attached to the property, but in the current short sale market, you will see more HELOCs (home equity line of credit). If a property goes into foreclosure, the second mortgage is wiped out, and the second lender will receive nothing. Second mortgages typically settle for $3,000 to $8,500 per deal, or $0.10 to $0.15 cents on the dollar. Remember, the loan in first lien position will generally allow a smaller payoff to junior lien holders, so the junior lien holder's options are limited. About 99 percent of second mortgages are at a zero-equity position in the property in this market. These typically are not too difficult to deal with, although advocates may run into a few bumps in the process here and there. The bottom line for the junior lien holders is they understand their position in the foreclosure process and that they will be wiped out at foreclosure. Therefore, they will take what they can get in most cases. Please note that while the chances are highly unlikely that a true second lien can come after a borrower after a foreclosure sale, they have every right to as long as the borrower is in a recourse state. If they were to follow through on this, they would technically have to sue the borrower. Truthfully, banks in junior positions generally are not going to invest in a legal pursuit of collection because many borrowers will file bankruptcy if they are pursued. More recently, I have seen the first lien position holder demand that the second position holder release the borrower from liability in exchange for the settlement payoff in the short sale. The vast majority of lenders in this position will send the seller a 1099-C to write off the loss.

Home Equity Line of Credit (HELOC): This is more like a credit card and needs to be negotiated for a settlement in order for the client to get a full release from this debt. Unlike a true second mortgage, if a foreclosure were to take place on the property, the bank/lender who issued the HELOC still maintains the right to collect for the debt owed even after foreclosure, whereas the true second mortgage is completely wiped out at foreclosure. Their lien on the title of the property will be gone, but their rights to collect on the deficiency will not. The main difference is HELOC debt is a collectible debt after foreclosure sale. Having the future debt obligation of a HELOC is another reason not to walk away and let the property foreclose. In this case, not only do those borrowers have a foreclosure on their credit, but they also have the full amount owed on the HELOC as a collectible balance plus a potential tax liability on unpaid debt. HELOCs right now are generally getting settled for about ten to twenty cents on the dollar. Smaller local banks will demand more. Therefore, use this as a guideline. A true second lien can sue for the difference, but will rarely do so. A HELOC doesn't have to sue for the difference. Their rights are already retained due to the characteristics of the loan. This is an important detail that borrowers with HELOCs must be familiar with.

Homeowners in trouble with a HELOC need to be made aware of the consequences of the HELOC if the property were to go into foreclosure. The main difference is for a true second to come after you, they have to go through the hassle of suing someone, whereas a HELOC's right never goes away—unless that same borrower subsequently files bankruptcy. Banks will typically sell this right to some collection company, which can be much more difficult to deal with.

D) WHAT IS A DEED IN LIEU OF FORECLOSURE?

This is considered a foreclosure prevention option and is often pushed by the banks. Essentially, a deed in lieu of foreclosure is just handing over the keys to the bank. This gives the bank the opportunity to take title (ownership) of the house without proceeding with the foreclosure. If the borrower gives the house back to the bank, the bank does not have to follow the state timelines for foreclosure. Worse yet, the word "foreclosure" will then appear on the borrower's credit report, and future lenders will treat the use of this option as a foreclosure.

A Deed in Lieu of Foreclosure Is a Great Option...*for the Bank*

It saves the bank thousands in hiring attorneys for a foreclosure. The home borrower may receive a letter for handing over the keys that says the bank will not pursue any unpaid debt. There are much better options that allow the borrower facing foreclosure to exit gracefully and not have the word "foreclosure" on his or her credit.

E) WHAT IS A LOAN MODIFICATION?

The definition of a loan modification is utilizing the existing mortgage company to refinance the debt or extend the terms of the loan. This may allow the home-owner to catch up at a more affordable level. To qualify, you must prove to the bank you have enough income to qualify for a loan modification. Most loan modifications will reduce your monthly payments with lower interest rates, and the bank adds any unpaid debt to your loan balance. However, in about 1 percent of cases, the bank may reduce your loan balance to make the payments more affordable.

How Tough Is It to Get a Loan Modification?

I do not think I have talked to anyone who said it was easy. The biggest challenge to most home borrowers is the qualification to a loan modification. The income requirements are very strict. You may not qualify if you do not make enough money—your debt-to-income ratio is too high. And you may not qualify if you make too much money. Often banks lose documents borrow-ers provide to them. Many people get strung along into thinking the loan modification is going forward, only to find the foreclosure still looms on the horizon. Some of the people who have had success told me it took as long as three to four years to get approved.

Trial Loan Modification – Is This Really Happening?

When a borrower applies for a loan modification, most banks will prequalify the borrower to start. The bank will then require the borrower to make "temporary payments" of a reduced amount. Those temporary payments are typically less than the typical mortgage payment needed to cover the debt, and are always lower than the final payment a borrower will have to pay if his or her loan modification is approved. While the borrower is making those temporary payments, the bank will continue to process the foreclosure. So, if the borrower does not get approved, after paying those payments, the bank has collected some money.

Permanent Loan Modification – The Holy Grail for Borrowers in Default...Or Is It?

If a loan modification is approved for a permanent recast, or refinance, of the mortgage, the borrower essentially starts over with a new loan. That new loan has a *higher* balance than they previously owed (banks add on missed payments and closing fees), and the borrower's interest rate may be a bit lower. Although most people want to stay in their homes, for some, this may not be the best financial decision. Many people find that if they choose another option, such as a short sale, they can buy a different home at a lower price in as little as one to three years, they are much better off financially, *and* most end up with a better home.

Case Study 3: Do Loan Modifications Really Work?

Government analysts report that only 7-15% of the loan modification applications actually get approved for a complete loan modification. In the meantime, the bank collects "temporary' payments" you will never get credit for...regardless of whether your loan modification is approved or not. Worse yet, the re-default rate after loan modification is a whopping 60 percent! That sounds like a huge number, and it is. Many factors go into that number, such as the economy and the job market. I also think the banks may be giving out loan modifications that are ultimately unaffordable for borrowers. Yes, the motivation of those owners to stay in their homes is so strong, they agree to take on the debt and commit themselves to four years of fewer choices. So, even if you get a loan modification, the chances of having a short sale or foreclosure in your future are, sadly, very high.

My colleagues in the industry are reporting that people they are helping to do a short sale after they received a loan modification are discovering the banks have placed a "silent second mortgage" on their home that shows up as an unexpected surprise when they try to sell the home on a short sale. The silent second consists of the balance of unpaid missed payments—in addition to their mortgage.

*I know this case study may be disheartening to those who read it. Not only do more than 85 percent of people who apply for loan modifications fail, but the few who get approved are still not better off financially. To those who are thinking of applying for a loan modification, consider the whole picture before you give the banks all of your financial information. It may make more sense to short sale off the mountain of unaffordable debt and purchase another, better home at a lower price with a low interest rate in just a few years. As an example, I know a family who bought a home with no-money-down financing, a first mortgage for $500,000, and a second mortgage for $245,000 for a purchase price of $745,000 in 2004. That same home is now worth $390,000. They are close to retirement age. Even if they got a loan modification, there is no way they could ever pay back all of that debt. If they short sale their home now, and rent for two years, they could buy a better home with far less debt. Current estimates indicate a larger than normal amount of foreclosures are expected to continue through 2018. That means those great deals **will still be there** for* *borrowers who choose to short sale their homes now and subsequently buy more affordable homes in just a few short years.*

F) WHAT IS A SHORT SALE?

The term "short sale" is used in the real estate world to describe when a property is sold for less than is owed on it and the bank agrees to discount the loan payoff enough to cover all the selling expenses for the home loan borrower. The borrower does not have to be behind on his or her mortgage to be approved for a short sale. Typically, a short sale occurs when there is more debt owed against the property than the actual property is worth. The owner can't sell or refinance the property unless the mortgage or lien holders agree to accept a payment that is less than—or short of—the amount the borrower actually owes. A short sale is a foreclosure pre-vention option used when the borrower sells his or her home for less than what is owed and the value of the home is less than what is owed on the property.

Short Sale to Leaseback Program

This is a brand-new program, offered to qualified bor-rowers, allowing them to sell their home on a short sale and then stay in and rent back the same home for a more affordable market-value rent payment. The home is sold to an approved nonprofit organization after borrowers qualify for the program. They may rent the home for three years after the short sale, with an opportunity to extend after that period. The borrowers who are approved for this program will have to go through financial counseling and prepare to be homeowners again in the future. I find most homeowners facing foreclosure want to stay in their home, stay in the same community, and not be required to move. To find out if this program exists in your area, please contact the author's office at 888-571-4442 to locate a certified short sale leaseback agent.

G) WHAT IS A DEFICIENCY JUDGMENT?

Many people tend to ask, what happens to all the debt that is never paid back to the bank? The result of lenders taking less money than what they are owed is called a deficiency. There are several ways a lender can handle a deficiency amount. Some lenders may pursue legal action to obtain a deficiency judgment against the borrower for the bank's loss. Here is what can happen after a short sale is conducted.

- **Forgiveness**: A foreclosure may result in cancellation of debt income depending on whether the bank pursues a deficiency judgment. If the bank chooses not to pursue a deficiency judgment, or pursues the judgment unsuccessfully, the borrower may incur income tax liability for debt forgiveness.

- **1099 Tax Form—For "Stealth Income"**: Banks typically will choose to write off any unpaid debt that was not paid by a borrower by issuing a 1099. There are two types of 1099s used. The 1099-C, Cancellation of Debt, is typically issued by banks when a borrower completes a short sale. That borrower will usually be responsible for paying taxes on any unpaid debt as it if it were income. The 1099-A reports the sale of the property as the full amount of the bank's loss. Whether or not there was a capital gain on the sale depends on the borrower's current financial situation, the original basis (purchase price of the home), and several other tax calculations. In either case, the bank considers its loss as the borrower's gain, therefore making the unpaid debt essentially taxable. If you sell the home while the 2007 Mortgage Debt Relief Act is still in effect, you may not have to pay taxes on the unpaid debt. If the home forecloses, another way to avoid paying taxes on unpaid debt is to claim insolvency when filing taxes. You should consult with a good attorney and/or tax professional about the debt obligations and tax implications of either case. Typically, foreclosed borrowers are obligated to pay back the debt, and usually have a debt burden of 10 to 20 percent *more* than if they would have sold their homes on short sales.

- **Promissory Note**: A bank can issue the borrower a promissory note that obligates the borrower to pay back the amount owed over an extended period of time, say fifteen to twenty years, in the form of monthly payments.

- **Cash Contribution**: Sometimes the banks may ask for extra cash at the time of closing, ranging anywhere from $200 to $5,000. This can be paid by the borrower or the buyer.

The options above are for banks to curb their losses. Since each situation is different, results will vary. The most important thing to remember is none of the debt remedies above is worse than having a foreclosure, in my opinion.

CHAPTER 2

INSIDER SECRETS TO A SUCCESSFUL SHORT SALE

Why Sell the Home on a Short Sale versus Other Foreclosure Prevention Options?

The answer is simple. Borrowers short sale their homes to avoid having to foreclose. Plus, the borrower who does a short sale has a lower debt and tax burden—oftentimes 100 percent of the unpaid debt can be wiped out for the borrower. A foreclosure has long-term and very adverse effects on a credit report. A short sale impacts the credit report only by showing late payments (if applicable) and lowering the credit score by about fifty points. It is reported as "paid as agreed," "paid as negotiated," or "settled." If the borrower happens to have an FHA loan and remains current on his or her mortgage during the course of a short sale, *that borrower can go buy another home using a new FHA loan, immediately after the short sale closes*!

A short sale is also another way for borrowers to stay in their homes longer than the foreclosure schedule (which is often delayed) while waiting for approval on the sale. During that time, borrowers can build a cash reserve to prepare to rent their next homes and start fresh, with less debt obligation, and rebuild their credit toward home ownership in the future.

Where Do I Start?

A short sale is conducted in a similar manner as a typical real estate sale. All banks require that a property be listed for sale by a real estate broker to get approval on a short sale. **You do not want just any real estate broker to handle a short sale**. Many brokers are afraid to help people with short selling their home because they are unfamiliar with how to get the right approval and help the borrowers in trouble. For the best results, it is recommended to hire a Certified Default Advocate who is also a real estate broker. A short sale is a complicated, highly specialized transaction that can have serious financial and tax ramifications. Borrowers in trouble who hire someone who does not understand how to get the appropriate short sale approvals from the bank risk having to pay more than they should of the debt or, worse yet, facing foreclosure. Many real estate brokers attempt to do a short sale for their clients without proper training—resulting in failure and the unsuspecting homeowner ending up with a foreclosure. Foreclosure while pursuing a short sale should not happen. That is why it is extremely important to hire the right real estate broker to handle a short sale.

Fortunately, current trends indicate the banks would prefer their borrowers do a short sale instead of a foreclosure. Banks have discovered they recover more money on their losses on a short sale than on a foreclosure. They have realized homes' values are higher when sold as a short sale rather than a foreclosure. Banks are very interested in neighborhood stabilization and improving market values, both of which are better for everyone. However, most banks will not take the time to train real estate agents on how to complete a successful short sale. The agent handling a short sale for a borrower needs to understand the process and prepare many things to complete a short sale and help the borrower avoid foreclosure. So, the choice a borrower in trouble makes when hiring a real estate broker is very important. It could mean the difference between being able to buy his or her next home in just a few years or having to wait as long as seven years to buy a home at higher prices and higher interest rates.

It is the real estate broker's job to bring in a purchaser for your home through aggressive and traditional marketing. Once an offer is received, the short sale approval process begins. However, before the process begins, it is essential the borrower and agent are ready to go with all the required documentation to submit a complete short sale package to the bank for approval. No lender will begin the process of a short sale without a full package being submitted. The banks often request documents from the borrowers facing foreclosure and requesting a short sale that are similar to making a loan application. They ask for current pay stubs, current bank statements, the previous two years of tax returns, a valid hardship letter, and a financial statement—as a minimum.

What Documents Does a Borrower in Default Need to Provide?

Some banks have their own forms the borrower must sign. Below is a typical list of requested documents:

- **Authorization Letter:** This is a letter that allows your default specialist to speak to the lien holder on your behalf. Without it, the real estate agent cannot communicate with your lien holder.

- **Payoff Request:** This document allows the person handling the closing to order your current payoff amount. The payoff on the loan is important to know exactly how much the bank's loss will be so that the real estate agent can successfully negotiate the sale..

- **Hardship Letter:** This is the borrower's explanation of the hardship that caused the need to do a short sale. Typical approved reasons for short sales are job loss, excess debts, medical, relocation, death, divorce, or need for different housing—such as a larger or smaller home or a home with main-level living.

- **Pay Stubs (two most recent):** This is so the lien holder can see an accurate accounting of your monthly income.

- **Bank Statements (two months' most recent):** The bank does not care if you make money, but they do want to confirm that your deposits correspond with your paycheck stubs and that the money spent each month is substantiated with your financial worksheet.

- **Federal Tax Returns:** The previous two years' tax returns with all forms and schedules.

- **Financial Worksheet:** This is the document where the monthly financial picture is summarized for the lien holder.

- **Exclusive Listing Agreement:** This document is supplied by the listing agent and signed by the borrower and listing agent.

- **Real Estate Purchase Contract:** Once an accepted contract is received, the agent will provide a copy of the fully signed contract with all the attached addendums.

- **Estimated HUD:** A settlement statement to close the sale, which will show an estimation of all the closings costs and the amount the bank will net after the sale. The listing agent typically obtains this from the closer at the closing title company.

- **Loan Approval for the Buyer:** The lien holders (banks) require a copy of the buyer's loan pre-approval if the buyer is obtaining new financing.

- **Bank-Specific Addendums:** The lien holders (banks) will often issue their own addendums to the short sale where the parties state they are not related to each other or to the agents. The document often supplied by the bank is called a Short Sale Affidavit. It will have language that prohibits the new buyer from renting the home back to the seller after closing. At times, the lien holders will put language in those addendums that restrict the new buyer from selling the property within a short period of time (typically ninety days) or for a price above 120 percent of their purchase price at the sale. Often the language in these addendums threatens *criminal charges* if the affidavit is violated.

So Why Do the Lenders Want All This Information?

If the borrower has already missed payments, why do the banks request so much financial documentation about the borrower in default? It is very unlikely that borrower will obtain a new loan anytime soon. The reasons are twofold:

1. The banks are trying to find out if those borrowers have assets and money that would qualify them for a loan modification or that could bring the loan current.

2. It is more likely banks are collecting updated information about the borrower to sell the unpaid debt for future collection when their financial situation improves.

   a. Having the potential for a collection and tax burden is why borrowers in trouble need to hire a Certified Default Advocate who negotiates for them and ensures the short sale approval letter is written with a "deficiency waiver" in it, meaning any unpaid debt will not be the borrower's responsibility going forward.

So, is the information given to the banks so that it may be used against them? The answer is yes! This is why consulting with an advocate when evaluating foreclosure prevention options is important to the borrower's financial future.

Typical Short Sale and Foreclosure Avoidance Timeline

Once the offer is received and all documentation is gathered, the process flows as follows:

Zero to Thirty Days

- File submitted to the banks or companies who hold a mortgage or lien against the property.
- Bank verifies documents and file is assigned to a negotiator
- Bank orders broker price opinion or appraisal of value

Thirty to Sixty Days

- Bank evaluates value against offer
- Bank typically requests updated documentation
- Negotiations can take place for approved settlement.
- Written short sale approval letter is received
- Both buyer and seller have an opportunity to accept or decline short sale approval.

Sixty to Ninety Days

- Buyer proceeds with normal purchase items such as inspection, appraisal, and loan approval
- Final settlement approved by bank

- Closing takes place and if the full release of any liability to pay unpaid debt is received in the approval letter(s)...the borrower is free of the debt.

Phase One, Zero to Thirty Days, Explained

In the first thirty days, your real estate broker should make sure a full short sale package is sent to all of the banks and/or the companies who have a mortgage or lien on the home. The next step is the bank(s) will order a BPO (broker price opinion) or its own appraisal of value. A BPO is like an appraisal of a property submitted by a Realtor. It is this value of the property that will eventually determine the end sales price, *as everything will revolve around the bank's opinion of value*. Different lenders have different guidelines on short sales, but in general, the value submitted as the BPO will be a key factor in final sales price. Do not be surprised if the buyer's initial offer amount is countered by the bank. The bank often responds back to the requested approved offer at the full market value provided by their vendors. The real estate broker needs to communicate frequently with the bank to make sure the file being processed and any updated documents are provided in a timely manner.

> *Case Study 4: Why Is the Bank's Opinion of Value So Important?*
>
> *One of our Monument short sales was a very large home on two and a half lovely treed acres. We made sure we met the person doing the BPO to provide a copy of recent sales so he would have good valid information to assess the fair market value of the*

home. Most banks will negotiate on market value, but it depends on the market value trends in your area. The banks typically will pay all the closing costs, which are usually about 8 percent (including commission, taxes, buyer's closing costs, title insurance, and some HOA fees). Sometimes the vendors hired by banks to determine value will use the easiest comparable sales to assess value, while others may not use the most appropriate comparable sales (comps). If the bank hires an agent doing the BPO valuation, he or she may be paid only thirty to seventy-five dollars for their three hours of work. So some agents doing a BPO may not take the time to do a really good price opinion of what the real market value is of that home. Or, they are unaware of how to pick the right comps (using the appropriate criteria). There is no agent qualification to do a BPO valuation. The banks are looking for an objective, fair market value within their own parameters about what a comp (comparable sale) is. In this case in Monument, the listing agent was told by an appraiser the value would likely come in well below the list price because of its condition. To our surprise, the appraisal for the second mortgage lender came in $125,000 more than fair market value. So, for months we had an uphill battle convincing the second mortgage lender the home was not *worth more than $125,000 above fair market value. Through diligence and persistence, we updated the second lien holder with appropriate comparable sales, and we got that short sale closed. Many, many agents would have given up and let that home foreclose because they did not know what they needed to do. According to a Senior Vice President at Bank of America, the banks lose, on average, 19% more if the home forecloses rather than accepting a short sale. This is especially true for the second mortgage lender because they end up receiving nothing if the home forecloses. So, it is up to us to fight the variables in the short sale system to get to closing. It is possible for the real estate broker to challenge a bank's opinion of value more than once, and with great success. Most agents would not know to try to fight for the value and the sales price.*

Phase Two, Thirty to Sixty Days, Explained

Phase two of the short sale process consists of receiving the value of the BPO and working with all additional liens on the title. It is important during this stage that the real estate professional obtain short sale approval letters with favorable terms for the borrower. Remember, it is only an offer of mortgage assistance. The real estate broker should have exit strategies planned should the initial offer not work out. During this stage, the agent should be negotiating between the lender, buyer, and seller in terms of price of the subject property.

Phase Three, Sixty to Ninety Days, Explained

For phase three, the borrower should receive the payoff demand letter or the short sale approval(s) from all lenders. The real estate broker should make sure the buyer is willing ready and able to close on the property at this point, contingency-free. Short sale approvals are typically valid for only thirty days after receipt. That is why the real estate broker has to make sure the buyer is progressing toward closing on or before the deadline. Please note the terms offered in the short sale approval letter(s) give the borrower and the buyer an opportunity to accept, counter, or reject the bank's offer.

Understanding the Relationship with My Bank and My Broker—Who Is Working for Me?

As the market has changed, so have the policies and preferences of the banks. Home borrowers facing the threat of a foreclosure need to know who is on their side.

Is My Bank on My Side?

The banks are required to reach out and exhaust all options to avoid foreclosure. However, their primary duty and obligation is to be a debt collector for their "investors"—the people who gave them the money for the home loan. Some banks are very helpful and easy to work with, while others are not-so-nice debt collectors who will try to scare and intimidate borrowers into paying amounts that may not be required. Some banks, especially in junior lien positions, may be so aggressive in their collection tactics they cause the borrower to turn to other actions, such filing for bankruptcy to dissolve that debt. That latter is especially true with some lenders who give home equity lines of credit (HELOCs). Those loans are like credit card debt, which hold the home as collateral against the debt. In the state of Colorado, those lenders can come after the borrower for unpaid debt for as long as six years after a foreclosure. So, hiring a Certified Default Advocate real estate broker to help the borrowers negotiate off some or all of that debt is important to their future financial well-being.

Is My Real Estate Broker on My Side?

The short answer is, he or she better be. Most state rules require real estate brokers act in the best interest of their clients (otherwise known as "fiduciary duty"). Although they earn a commission if there is a sale, the commission is paid upon the successful negotiation of the short sale and paid by the bank. The real estate broker's, job is to inform borrowers of their options, help get the home sold for the highest value possible, and support the borrowers to make the best decisions for their families.

A real estate broker has no duty to the bank on the short sale, as the bank is not the real estate broker's client. Some less informed real estate brokers often confuse short sales with REOs (bank foreclosures, or "real estate owned"), and they think the bank is their client. Some agents also think the bank is the decision maker on the sale of the property. The seller in title is the owner and decision maker on the property all the way until the time the bank forecloses on it. Only the seller (owner of record) can accept, reject, and entertain offers. A short sale is only an approved payoff amount the bank is going to accept or deny to release their lien interest and, preferably, settle the debt that is owed to them by the seller. The seller owns the property. The bank owns the note attached as collateral for the debt against the property. The real estate broker works for the seller, not the bank. Only the seller can have the final say on the terms of the contract for sale, as well as whether they will accept the bank's offer as debt settlement on the sale.

According to RealtyTrac, as of September 2011, bank foreclosures sell for 39.92 percent under market value, while short sales sell for 20.51 percent under market value. The mere fact that the seller is participating in a short sale shows the bank (lien holder) the seller is working toward mitigating the bank's loss. Banks fully understand they lose less money approving a short sale (debt settlement) as compared to the losses they experience in a foreclosure. It takes the services of a Certified Default Advocate to successfully negotiate that debt settlement and help those homeowners in trouble avoid foreclosure.

Pricing the Property

During phase one of the short sale process, the banks will approve, counter, or not approve the agreed-upon sales price on your property based on their determined value of the home. So, it is best for the real estate broker to price the property appropriately in order to motivate a buyer to buy the home as close as possible to market value according to the borrower's current situation. If the borrower is not facing a foreclosure sale date, there might be more time to price the home at the high end of market value in order to get as much as possible for the home. If the foreclosure sale date is approaching soon, the pricing strategy will need to be more aggressive in order to obtain as many offers as possible in less time. In most cases, the borrower will not be held accountable for the unpaid debt.

Case Study 5: Run Silent, Run Deep—Toward Foreclosure

One of my clients had their home on the market with another agent (who rarely spoke to them) for almost two years expecting a retail sale. The retail sale the other agent promised just did not happen. During the course of the home being offered at a high (retail) price, Mr. Borrower lost his job and they could not make the payments. They contacted me for help. They had built this lovely home themselves and hoped this home would be their retirement home. However, when he lost his job, they could no longer afford the home. The huge house payments were impossible without a steady income. He did freelance work but the income was not enough to be approved for a loan modification. They wanted to continue living in the home during the foreclosure process to build any cash reserves they could. So the pricing strategy was to slowly work the sales price down until a suitable buyer for the home was found. That took about three months. And once we did get a good offer, the bank was willing to extend the foreclosure sale date until the short sale could be approved. The home closed two months after we received a buyer, and their short sale approval letter had a waiver of deficiency for both the first and second mortgages. That means they never had to pay back any unpaid debt, and because of the 2007 Mortgage Debt Relief Act, they never had to pay taxes on unpaid debt as if it were income.

Why Will the Bank "Forgive" My Debt?

Recently, banks have been under a lot of pressure from lawsuits, consumers, and investors about how they handle defaulting loans. Most banks are able to take the write-off of the debt by issuing a 1099-C. It costs money to collect the debt after a foreclosure. Due to the volume of defaulting borrowers and the cost to collect the debt, banks are more likely to forgive and/or write it off through the issuance of a 1099-C instead of collecting the debt into the future.

What Do I Do after a Short Sale?

After a short sale, the borrower is relieved of the stress of paying the house payments or making up any back payments. It's time to get back on track financially and to restore credit. Many people will rent for a while until their credit is fixed, and in just a few years, they can qualify to buy another house. With the right team of people and resources, that same borrower will be able to purchase another home as soon as two years later, on average. I have seen people who did a short sale purchase a much better home at a lower price in as little as one and a half years after the short sale.

How Much Money Does a Short Sale Cost Me?

There should be *no cost to the homeowner* for doing a short sale. The bank that holds the first position mortgage (usually the largest one) will provide a short sale approval letter, which will absorb all of the closing costs associated with selling a home by reducing the approved payoff of the first mortgage enough to cover all the closing costs. These costs include property taxes, title costs, attorney fees, tax assessments, payments to junior lien holders, real estate commission, and title fees. The banks will even approve covering the costs of the buyer's loan closing costs in most cases.

Do I Have to Fix Up My Home to Short Sell It?

Many people, understandably, have a wonderful sense of pride about the look of their homes when they put it up for sale. Yet, most home sellers facing foreclosure do not have the extra cash to fix up their homes. The short answer is no, short sale sellers do not have to fix up your home at all. However, if the borrower's home is located in areas where the pipes may freeze in the winter, it is advisable to have a plumber winterize the home before the utilities are shut off or the home is vacated. That way, the home will likely be protected from freeze damage and will command higher market value on the sale.

Case Study 6: The pipes froze with no funds to fix it

I met a nice young man who, sadly, had lost his mom recently. As he was getting ready to sell her home, he received a call from the water company informing him a lot of water was being used at the empty home. When he went over there, he found that the pipes had frozen and broken and caused thousands of gallons of water to damage the home inside. Fortunately, a friend referred him to a great real estate broker and he was able to sell the home to an investor without fixing a thing. He was so grateful for her help and relieved that there was no cost to sell the home and have the problem be handled by someone else.

CHAPTER 3

THE 2007 MORTGAGE DEBT FORGIVENESS ACT

When an advocate negotiates a short sale correctly, the borrower can expect to be given debt forgiveness in conjunction with receiving a 1099-C. The legislation that is in effect right now can best be summarized as follows: Any borrower who receives a 1099 resulting from a short sale is completely forgiven from any 1099 tax liabilities if the home was their primary residence. Since some exceptions apply, it is best to speak with your tax professional to determine if you qualify for debt cancellation.

Words of Caution for Those Thinking They May Have to Short Sell Their Homes

This very generous law is currently set to expire at the end of 2013. Borrowers who think their home may end up as a foreclosure this year should not delay in taking action to settle the issue before the end of 2013. Many promised loan modifications never come true. Many short sales take longer than expected. It is highly recommended that borrowers facing foreclosure who dream of a loan modification or think they may have trouble selling their home seriously consider the short sale option as soon as possible. Once this law expires, if borrowers then elect to do a short sale, they may be held accountable to pay taxes on any unpaid debt issued in the form of a 1099-C.

So, as an example, if the bank's losses on a short sale are, say, $75,000, the bank issues a 1099-C for $75,000 of income the borrower never received. Then the borrower may be liable to pay approximately $15,000 in taxes on that debt reported as income for that borrower.

IRS debt *cannot* be charged off. Nor can you file bankruptcy to get rid of IRS debt. The government is relentless in their collection efforts. They will not stop filing liens, garnishing wages, taking tax returns, disallowing new loans, and destroying credit until they get their money.

CHAPTER 4

HOW DOES A FORECLOSURE OR SHORT SALE AFFECT MY CREDIT?

If a borrower has to foreclose on a home, his or her credit will be affected for about seven-plus years. When a borrower sells the home on a short sale, the credit is also affected, but for a much shorter time period, and less damage is done. Typically, the credit score of a borrower who elects to do a short sale is affected by a reduction of 50 to 100 points. The impact of a foreclosure is about 250 to 300 points off the score. Every person has his or her own FICO, and each individual's score will vary. Most people are usually able to qualify for a new loan and buy a new home within two to three years after a short sale, versus the wait of four to seven years to buy another home if a borrower were to let the home foreclose. Since everyone is different, it's best to consult with a credit-repair person or your real estate professional in more detail.

Potential Consequences for the Various Options

- **Short Sale Reporting:** When a short sale is completed, it will show up on the credit report as:
    - "Paid account/zero balance settlement accepted on this account. Settled: less than full balance"
    - The good news is, that after about two to three years, the credit score will come right back up. Many people end up buying another home in as little as two years after a short sale.

- **Deed in Lieu of Foreclosure Reporting:** If the home is handed over in a deed in lieu of foreclosure, the report will show the word "foreclosure." Therefore, future mortgage lenders will view it as a foreclosure.
    - Wait time for next home: four to seven years

- **Foreclosure Reporting:** If the home forecloses, the report will likely say:
    - "Credit grantor reclaimed collateral to settle defaulted mortgage. Foreclosure, real estate mortgage."
    - Wait time for next home: four to seven years

Case Study 7: The Road Back to Prosperity— Sooner Than You Think

Although these past few years have seen a substantial reduction in market values, in most markets today, home values are starting to rise. Many people who had to short sale or foreclose had loans with high interest rates, or loans with rates that adjusted and caused their house payments to rise while the market values declined below what they owed on the home. For some, that was true even after they put down large cash payments on the home. According to RealtyTrac, the volume of borrowers who are facing difficulty will continue until 2018. **What may shock many people is that borrowers who received a loan modification cannot refinance or purchase a home with a new loan for four years.** *Yet many borrowers can buy another home after a short sale in as little as two to three years. There are some exceptions made to the time from short sale to the next purchase. I know of a few homeowners who were able to buy another home in less than two years. So, those same people who had to short sale their homes are able to buy homes sooner and enjoy low fixed interest rates and low home prices. The last time it was less expensive to buy a home than rent was 1974. Homebuyers and investors are buying homes all over the country because they know home values will continue to rise as they have for the last forty years (excepting the last four years). There has never been a better time than now to invest in real estate.*

CHAPTER 5

WILL FILING BANKRUPTCY HELP ME?

When faced with foreclosure, many people think that turning to bankruptcy will allow them to cancel their debt and keep their homes. Filing for bankruptcy can help borrowers consolidate debt payments and wipe out liabilities on unsecured debt and even some junior lien holders. It depends on the type of bankruptcy the borrower files for as to whether it may help them with the foreclosure. Often people are too hasty to file bankruptcy and the result may be *both* a bankruptcy *and* a foreclosure.

There are 2 types of bankruptcy most often used when facing foreclosure:

Chapter 7 – Cancels most personal debt. But it does not apply to mortgage debt because the debt is secured by the collateral of the house. So, if the mortgage is not paid and the chapter 7 completed the mortgage company can file a petition to continue with the foreclosure.

Chapter 13 -This type of bankruptcy lets you pay of the back payments, over a length of time, usually five years. In this case, the borrower would need enough income to at least meet the current mortgage payment and the amount of the back payments.

If a borrower plans to eventually sell a property as a short sale after bankruptcy, the banks can pick up right where they left off in the foreclosure process and foreclose on the home immediately after it is released from the bankruptcy. In other words, if the borrower was 90 days into a 120-day pending foreclosure, with 30 days left, the bank can start at 30 days left from the time the home is released from the bankruptcy. Trying to conduct a short sale while in bankruptcy to stop the foreclosure process will just delay the foreclosure and stop the short sale. A bankruptcy only temporarily slows the foreclosure—unless the borrower plans to pay back the bank for unpaid payments over time. The bankruptcy has to be discharged or the property has to be exempted from the bankruptcy in order to conduct a short sale.

A bankruptcy will stay on the borrower's credit report, and for most, bankruptcy is very emotionally upsetting. My best advice on this subject is to consult with an excellent bankruptcy attorney to discuss the options. I have seen some homeowners file bankruptcy because they had so many other debts that they needed a clean slate. One key point to keep in mind is if the home is the only debt that is creating an unmanageable situation for the borrower, then a short sale option may be a better choice than bankruptcy and far less damaging on the credit reporting over all.

CHAPTER 6

SPECIAL HELP FOR ACTIVE-DUTY MILITARY MEMBERS

As a retired navy reserve officer, and having grown up in an air force family, military people hold a very special place in my heart. They are not easily given the opportunity to purchase a home and stay in it for fifteen to thirty years until it is paid off. The military, as a practice, requires its members to move very often around the world to meet the needs of its services and to defend the freedom that our civilian population enjoys. Yet many military members choose to buy homes, and may plan to keep them only for a few years, or keep them long-term and return to those homes when they complete their careers in the military.

The Problem

The recent correction (reduction) in housing values caused many military members to be stuck with homes that were worth less than what they owed on them. Few military members have enough cash reserves to pay the difference if their home is not worth what they owe and they need to sell it due to being assigned a different duty location.

The option of renting out the home until the market improves comes with many risks, such as tenants destroying the property and not making their monthly rent payments. Having a home as a rental property and living far away is a risk few military members want to take.

Another huge dilemma is the threat of military members losing their security clearances if they are left with no choice but to miss mortgage payments or, even worse, let the home foreclose. The consequences of their credit score going down could mean the loss of their security clearance, resulting in the loss of their military position or being required to leave the service before they are eligible for retirement.

Solutions

Finally, after four years of military members becoming some of the hardest hit segments of the population with the housing correction, the Veterans Administration and banks have developed some excellent options to help our military gracefully avoid foreclosure and credit damage.

Option 1: Military Loan Modification

Some banks, such as Bank of America, offer a special loan modification for military members:

> *Bank of America's Military Loan Modification Program builds on the government's Home Affordable Modification*

Program (HAMP), and provides military service members with principal reduction measures as determined by HAMP guidelines. Military mortgage reduction measures include immediate forgiveness on the principal, to reduce mortgage debt to as low as 100 percent of the current market value. Since April 1, 2011, Bank of America also offers a reduced 4 percent interest rate on mortgages for active-duty military personnel who are eligible for Service members Civil Relief Act (SCRA) protection, which is applicable during the borrowers' active-duty service and for 12 months after separation. Also included is a loan-term extension, to help military service members arrive at a more affordable monthly mortgage payment.

If military members are not financed through Bank of America, and they want to keep their homes, I recommend they contact their banks and ask them if there is a program that they offer to military members.

One thing I learned while I was in the military is you have to ask a lot of questions to get the answers you need. More and more recently, most banks that I deal with on a daily basis ask me if my clients are active-duty military members because they do offer special programs for them.

Option 2: The "Compromised Sale" for VA Loans

This is essentially a short sale for military members who obtained their financing through a VA loan. The great news is the borrower *does not* have to miss payments to do a "compromised sale." They just need to show PCS orders. The potential consequence to the borrower is that their VA eligibility may not be 100 percent available if they do a compromised sale after obtaining a VA loan. Their VA eligibility can be used again after this type of sale. However, it may limit their purchasing loan amount for their next home. This calculation is somewhat complicated, so I recommend that military members contact their regional Veterans Affairs office and ask to speak to a VA loan specialist. My regional VA loan specialist tells me that some banks waive the reduction of the military member's VA loan eligibility after the compromised sale, which fully reinstates that borrower's ability to use his or her VA in the future. The VA loan specialist told me the veteran can find out find out what eligibility remains about two months after the compromised sale. And, that same borrower can use his or her VA soon after the compromised sale.

Option 3: The Short Sale with Military Benefits

This is recent news and very important to military borrowers who are facing a housing hardship. Nearly all banks are offering special incentives to borrowers to help with relocation expenses *and* avoid foreclosure. Most have a policy, and it is law that they will not foreclose on active-duty members because of the Service members Civil Relief Act (SCRA). However, it does happen. Military members need to work with the banks and their military legal departments to fight for their legal rights. You should know the banks are more motivated than ever to prevent foreclosure, and they do not want to be sued for faulty foreclosure—especially for active-duty military members.

Special Relocation Incentives for Active-Duty Members:

Banks are very patriotic. Most of the large banks are now offering a relocation incentive to active military borrowers who have **PCS** orders. I've heard some active duty members are receiving *as much as $20,000* in relocation incentive for short selling their homes upon transfer orders. However, the military member needs to hire a Certified Default Advocate who knows how to request this incentive.

Considerations for Military Members with Security Clearances

Having held a security clearance while I served, and having had a discussion with my security office about the housing crisis, I am hopeful this advice is helpful.

- If the military member has Permanent Change of Station (PCS) orders and can manage continuing to make house payments for a few months while his or her Certified Default Advocate helps sell the home, it is best to continue to make those payments and best to continue to keep the utilities on or have the home winterized to protect the pipes from freezing during the winter months. The further in advance they prepare for this, the better.

Case Study 8: Soldier Had to Short Sale His Home, Stayed Current on the Debt, and Kept His Security Clearance

I helped a young family who had orders from Fort Carson, Colorado, to Korea. They did not think they would be moving back to Colorado or retiring in the area after his service ended. For months, we tried to sell their home at a price enough to pay off the mortgage. However, we did not receive an offer that would allow for a full payoff. The biggest concern of these borrowers was the credit damage because the military member held a security clearance. As their Certified Default Advocate, I coordinated with their bank and determined they could sell their home for less than what they owed at no cost to them and continue to make house payments to protect their credit rating. Once they decided to do a compromised sale, things moved fairly quickly. We priced the home appropriately, and they received six offers, then selected the highest one. In just six weeks, their sale was approved by the bank, and we closed three weeks later. During that time, their transfer orders came through, and they moved to Korea. They only had to make one month's house payment during the move. It was a happy day for me to tell that family their sale was closed without a problem and they did not have to worry about any unpaid mortgage debt. All of the unpaid debt was forgiven, in writing. Plus, they will still be able to use their VA loan eligibility when they choose to do so.

- If the military member can no longer afford payments, be sure to communicate the issue to the security office.

I have had both active-duty military members and civilian employees with a clearance coordinate with their security office about the issue with no impact to the clearance status. The security offices have recently become more forgiving to borrowers who have potential issues with late mortgage payments because the problem is so widespread. The military member is always better off, though, to keep his or her security office informed about the situation and what is being done to correct it, such as the options offered in this book. According to Fannie Mae, "on its own, a short sale does not challenge most security clearances."

- Military members should not wait until the last minute to resolve the issue of not being able to pay mortgage payments. Per the Soldiers and Sailors Civil Relief Act, banks are not supposed to be foreclosing on active-duty members. However, it has happened in the past four years. Base legal should be consulted about the issues as soon as possible. Having adverse marks placed on the credit report while holding a security clearance could have an impact on a military member's ability to keep his or her clearance. The banks are supposed to remove those adverse credit marks. However, the military member has to fight the banks to remove adverse credit reporting at times. It is always best to "communicate, communicate, communicate" early.

- I attend many conferences about what banks call "the Default Industry" where they repeatedly say the borrower is much better off dealing with the issue early in the process rather than later in the process. Plus, banks are much more willing to provide cash relocation incentives for homeowners who work to solve the issues early in the process.

CHAPTER 7

THE SEVEN THINGS YOU MUST KNOW TO AVOID FORECLOSURE

1. **Discuss Your Options with Certified Default Advocate** *before* **you call your bank:** Remember, everything borrowers tell the bank can and will be used against them. The banks do record their phone calls, and they keep excellent notes of conversations. Talk to a Certified Default Advocate first, and find out about the options for your situation.

2. **Learn all of your options before you talk to the bank.** There are some excellent resources online, such as www.MakingHomeAffordable.gov, and the Web sites of your own banks. This book also gives some great information about the options.

3. **Protect your assets.** The banks will try to collect the money borrowers have to make mortgage payments. Build a separate savings account to help with the next planned move. Banks will ask for copies of the

borrower's bank statements and pay stubs. They are looking to see that their mortgage holders are not millionaires and that they have a valid hardship. Borrowers in trouble will need some cash reserves to be approved to rent the next home. It is very risky to have checking and savings accounts with the same bank that holds the mortgage. I have heard of many cases where that same bank just drains people's checking account to pay the mortgage without notice. Some banks have fine print in their mortgage paperwork that gives them the authority to drain the borrower's checking account to make the house payment when mortgage payments are not made.

4. **The risk of deed in lieu of foreclosure:** Banks are skilled at selling this program as a "graceful exit." Make no mistake about it—a feed-in-lieu of foreclosure is a foreclosure wolf in sheep's clothing, in my opinion. The banks make this option very attractive by putting in writing that they will not collect on the debt into the future. But a deed in lieu of foreclosure places the word "foreclosure" on a credit report and prevents that borrower from buying another home for at least four years. There are better options that are not so harmful to credit that allow borrowers in trouble to buy another home sooner, while the prices and interest rates are low.

5. **Options for temporary hardships:** It is OK to ask the bank about the Home Affordable Unemployment Program. For eligible borrowers, the mortgage payment may be temporarily reduced to no more than 31 percent

of their monthly income for three to twelve months. If unemployment is not the issue, a forbearance agreement, where they break up the missed payments across six to eight months and add that amount to the regular payments so the borrower can catch up on missed payments, maybe also be requested. This is an option that the borrower must request. Sometimes that request must be made at the supervisor level. Typically, banks will approve this request if the borrower is less than ninety days delinquent on payments.

6. **Do I have to miss payments to get a loan modification or sell my home on a short sale?** The short answer is no. As long as borrowers have a valid hardship, such as loss of income, potential imminent default, relocation, divorce, or a change in family status that mandates a need for different housing, they may be approved for short sales without missing payments. This is particularly important for those people who must maintain a good credit score to keep their jobs and/or security clearances.

7. **Ask for Relocation Money:** Most banks have their own programs in addition to government programs. Relocation Incentives range from $1,000 to $45,000 in "relocation incentive" when borrowers chose to sell their home on a short sale.

CHAPTER 8

OPTIONS WHEN FACING FORECLOSURE

- **Do Nothing**

If homeowners do nothing, they most likely will lose their homes at foreclosure sale. When that person make an application on just about any loan applications in the future, the lender will ask if the applicant has ever had a foreclosure.. The word "Foreclosure" will stay on a person's credit report for about 7 years. Sadly, a majority of defaulted borrowers choose to let the bank take the home and foreclose on them.

- **Payoff Request**

Completely pay off the entire loan amount plus any default amount and fees. Usually this is accomplished through a refinance of the debt. New debt is normally at a higher interest rate, and there may be a prepayment penalty because of the recent default. With this option, there should be equity in the home.

- **Reinstatement**

This is repaying the entire amount of missed payments plus interest, attorney fees, late fees, taxes, missed payments, and fees to bring the loan current again.

- **Loan Modification**

A loan modification is a recast (or refinance) of the current mortgage, possibly at lower payments. Most banks, if the borrower is approved, will:

- o Reduce the interest rate
- o Restructure the loan from an interest-only to a fully amortized loan, or
- o Reduce the principal
- o Most will add any back payments onto the current loan balance.
  - If the borrower receives a loan modification approval, he or she needs to keep an eye out for those sneaky "silent second mortgages." Silent second mortgages are placed on homes by banks who lump the missed back payments and fees into a second mortgage without the borrower signing second mortgage documents, and require collection if the borrower sells the home.

- **Forbearance**

A lender may be able to arrange a repayment plan based on the homeowner's financial situation. The lender may even be able to provide a temporary payment reduction or suspension of payments. Information will be required by the lender to show that the homeowner is able to meet the new payment plan requirements. This can be an excellent option for people who want to stay in their homes and have the resources to make up a few back payments over about a six-month period.

- **Partial Claim**

This is a loan from the initial lender, for a second loan to include back payments, costs, and fees.

- **Deed in Lieu of Foreclosure**

Give the property back to the bank instead of the bank foreclosing. Banks generally require that the home be well maintained, and taxes must be current. It is viewed, on the credit report, by future lenders as a foreclosure.

- **Bankruptcy**

This option can liquidate debt and/or allow more time. As far as home mortgage debt is concerned, it will delay foreclosure. However, a bankruptcy does not stop the bank from foreclosing after the bankruptcy discharged (completed). It is best to speak to a qualified bankruptcy attorney regarding this subject.

- **Short Sale**

This is when a property is sold for less than is owed on it and the bank agrees to a discounted payoff. If the property has equity (money left over after all loans and monetary encumbrances are paid), the homeowner may sell the home without lender approval through a routine home sale when the bank's liens are fully paid off at closing. On the other hand, a short sale can be negotiated with the bank if the total of the bank's liens exceed the property's value. The benefits of a short sale outweigh letting it foreclose, doing a deed in lieu of foreclosure, or bankruptcy. This is the shortest path back to home ownership again, with the least damage to the borrower's credit score. My company has helped hundreds of borrowers having trouble staying in their homes to sell their homes for less than what they owe! Nearly all have received a complete release from paying back any unpaid debt or taxes on any unpaid debt.

- **Short Sale Leaseback**

Homeowners who qualify for this program may sell their home on a short sale to an approved nonprofit investor, and be able to lease back the same home for at least three years at current market rental rates.

CHAPTER 9

TOP FIVE FEARS WHEN FACING FORECLOSURE—ANSWERED

Fear 1: My bank wants to foreclose.

False. A foreclosure is bad for everyone. The home's condition will likely be degraded by a foreclosure. Examples are the homes' heat is shut off and pipes break, pools turn green, homes get broken into and the built-in appliances and light fixtures are taken, and the landscaping dies. The neighborhood values tend to decrease if there are a lot of foreclosures in the neighborhood. The banks usually lose more money as a result of a foreclosure. Worst of all, families are very negatively impacted by foreclosures—not only by negative credit reporting but by the difficulties families have in staying together through a financial crisis.

Fear 2: My neighbors know when I miss payments.

False. Neighbors do not know about the financial situation of their neighbors.

Fear 3: The sheriff will kick me out of the home when I miss payments.

False. Missing home payments means the borrower has defaulted on the loan. The banks can file for foreclosure from the time the first payment is missed. However, most banks do not start the process that soon. The banks will typically start official foreclosure process anywhere from three months to twenty-four months after missed payments. After the banks file for foreclosure there is usually a time delay before they can take ownership of the property. In the state of Colorado, where my business is based, it takes at least another 120 days before the foreclosure is complete. After the foreclosure sale, the bank's attorney would have to file an eviction in the courts to make the homeowner move. Eviction often takes one to three months—after the foreclosure. Notice must be sent to the borrower about both the foreclosure process starting and any eviction proceedings after the foreclosure.

> *Case Study 9: The Bank Told a Lady Her Possessions Would Be Thrown Out in Two Days If She Did Not Make Up Her Two Missed Payments Immediately.*
>
> *I called one borrower facing foreclosure, and she informed me her bank told her if she did not pay her two missed house payments that day, they would come and throw her stuff out on the street in two days! I was both angry at the bank and heartbroken for the homeowner when I heard this. This threat was made by an employee of a large major bank that*

is no longer in business. Not only was that statement, made by an unscrupulous bank employee, completely untrue, and not consistent with state law, it is against the Federal Fair Debt Collections Act to intimidate a borrower with false statements. She moved her family that weekend. **The bank foreclosed on that same home—three years later!**

Fear 4: After a foreclosure or a short sale, I can never buy a home again.

False. In as little as one to three years from short selling a home, borrowers can buy another home. If the borrower forecloses, it could take as long as seven years to buy another home. Sometimes even the same banks will lend you money again as long as you improve your credit standing after the foreclosure or short sale.

A word of caution about accepting a loan modification. Borrowers cannot get another mortgage until *after four years* of accepting a loan modification. So borrowers must think about whether that loan modification will really be a blessing or not, as 60 percent of borrowers re-default after accepting a loan modification.

Fear 5: I will have to pay back my financial obligations on any unpaid debt or pay taxes on unpaid debt.

The requirement to pay back mortgage debt after a short sale is very unlikely. Right now, for the home as a primary residence, borrowers who short sale their homes will not have to pay taxes on any unpaid debt that is written off in the form of a 1099-C. This law, however, is set to expire at the end of 2013. Most industry experts believe this law may be extended in the current market environment.

Most lenders are willing to issue short sale approval letters with a waiver of any "deficiency" of unpaid debt. That means, when they put it in writing, they cannot collect for any unpaid debt into the future. This is the best solution, and the one we always seek as Certified Default Advocates. The exception may be with the junior lien holders. Many second mortgages and home equity lines of credit are less inclined to waive the deficiency. That is why it is so important for a borrower facing foreclosure to hire a good Real Estate Broker and Certified Default Advocate who knows how to negotiate with the banks to obtain written release of the debt upon the completion of a short sale.

CHAPTER 10

WHAT THE EXPERTS HAVE TO SAY ABOUT THE FUTURE OF REAL ESTATE INVESTING

From the end of 2011 through the end of 2012, the market values of homes actually went up in value in most areas of the country. Yet in many markets, the real estate values had dropped so radically, borrowers who are upside down on their values have still not seen their home's market values rise enough to meet the debt obligations against their homes. The government has added a few new programs to help those people refinance their homes if they are current on their mortgages, such as the Home Affordable Refinance Program (HARP). Those programs are helpful but will not stem the tide of people who took on loans that will increase in payments because of a five-year adjustable-rate mortgage over the next several years. Industry experts think the volume of short sales and foreclosures will continue for another five to seven years from now. According to Daren Blomquist of RealtyTrac, of the 42.1 million homeowners with loans, 10.9 million are "underwater" (in value) on their mortgage. With market values trending up in most areas, there are still at least five-plus years to go before some of those homeowners have positive equity in their homes. Market values are expected to rise only slowly over the next several years.

All across the country, investors are buying the best deals on the market as quickly as they can. Money typically flows toward the best perception of value. Those investors are keeping homes for rentals, as well as fixing up homes to sell for a profit. It is encouraging to know investors think this is a great time to buy real estate.

I recently heard of another factor, with regard to population demographics, from demographic specialist Harry Dent. He indicates it will be at least seven years before the "Millennial Generation" will come of age to contribute to the economy in the form of buying homes and increasing their net worth. People peak in their spending years at age forty-six. There are seventy-eight million Baby Boomers whose peak spending years were in the 1990s. There were only forty-five million Generation Xers whose peak spending years are between 2010 and 2020. We can look forward to the prosperity of the eighty million Millennials, young people born between 1980 and 2006, who will start reaching their peak years at the end of this decade. The size of the Millennial Generation is even larger than the Baby Boom Generation. Experts say our market's economy, politics and government spending aside, will grow very quickly during the years the Millennial Generation matures, starting in 2020. So hug those Millennial kids. They do represent a brighter future for everyone.

Case Study 10: The Road to Prosperity Again

As I was completing this book, I was thrilled to have two of my former short sale sellers contact me (in the same week!) to let me know they are ready to buy another home. It is such great news to know they can buy a home now at the low interest rates and prices. Best of all, their monthly payments will be lower than what they are paying in rent!

IN CONCLUSION

It is my hope and mission that this information will help people better understand their options when house payments become unaffordable. It is important borrowers discuss their particular situation with a Certified Default Advocate since all situations differ. My staff is available for a free, private, no-obligation consultation to discuss the available options. Even if we are not located close to your area, we can find a Certified Default Advocate who can help. If you have questions, please reach us directly at 888-571-4442. Best wishes, and thank you for reading this book.

ABOUT THE AUTHOR

Barb Schlinker is a Certified Default Advocate who has helped hundreds of homeowners buy and sell homes. She specializes in helping homeowners in default avoid foreclosure. Barb is a retired Navy Reserve Officer. She holds a Bachelor's Degree in Professional Aeronautics and an Associate's Degree in Business. Barb opened Parker St Claire Realty in October 2004. Barb is also the editor and publisher of three local real estate newspapers: Springs Real Estate News, Fountain Real Estate News and Monument Real Estate News. Her experience in training helping people avoid foreclosure is vast. She received her short sale training from the former Senior Indy Mac Loss Mitigator – Mr. Lee Honish and has obtained certifications such as Certified Default Advocate, Certified Distressed Property Expert and Master Default Intermediary.

CDAT • CDPE CERTIFIED DISTRESSED PROPERTY EXPERT • VAREP VETERANS ASSOCIATION OF REAL ESTATE PROFESSIONALS • SSLB

MDI

REO4KIDS.COM

Email: ColoradoBarb@Gmail.com
Websites: www.ColoradoBarb.com
http://www.ColoradoSpringsShortSale.com

www.ingramcontent.com/pod-product-compliance
Lightning Source LLC
Chambersburg PA
CBHW060637210326
41520CB00010B/1635